The Big Scoop!

Best Sensational Sorbet Recipes - Dairy-Free Desserts to Make at Home

BY

Daniel Humphreys

W0010626

License Notes

No part of this Book can be reproduced in any form or by any means including print, electronic, scanning or photocopying unless prior permission is granted by the author.

All ideas, suggestions and guidelines mentioned here are written for informative purposes. While the author has taken every possible step to ensure accuracy, all readers are advised to follow information at their own risk. The author cannot be held responsible for personal and/or commercial damages in case of misinterpreting and misunderstanding any part of this Book

Table of Contents

Introduction

There is basically one key ingredient that makes the difference between ice cream and sorbet and that is milk. The former has it, the latter doesn't. To make the perfect sorbet all you need is sugar, water, and a little fruit.

Plus of course, sorbet has been around a lot longer than ice-cream. The first known record of ice being combined with fruit was in China over 3000 years ago. While the Mesopotamians have the honor of being the first to serve wine, mixed with ice or snow, as far back as the 5th century, BC.

The Ancient Egyptians got in on the act too, with nobles offering their guests a silver chalice filled half with fruit and half with ice.

But it was the Romans who created sorbets prepared with ice, fruit and honey. In fact, European folklore claims that sorbet was invented by Nero during the first century AD.

The Roman Emperor is said to have had slaves along the Via Appia Antica (the road from Rome to Brindisi) pass buckets full of snow hand over hand from the mountains, direct to the tables of his banqueting halls. When it arrived, it was then combined with local wine and raw honey.

Today, sorbet is the perfect dessert for food lovers; enjoyed as a between-course palate cleanser. While those watching their weight can indulge in this treat knowing that most recipes are free of fat, dairy, cholesterol and of course – guilt!

OVER 21's

Apple and Calvados Sorbet

A palate cleansing sorbet popular in Normandy and Brittany, where it is generally served in between courses.

Servings: 8-10

Total Time: 2hours 45mins

Ingredients:

- 1⅓ cup sharp apples (peeled, chopped)
- 3 cups cold water
- ½ cup white sugar
- ¼ cup freshly squeezed lemon juice
- ¼ tsp lemon zest
- ¼ cup Calvados

Directions:

1. Using a medium sized saucepan, combine the apple, cold water and white sugar. Bring to a simmer. Cover the pan with a tight fitting lid and reduce the heat a little. Allow the mixture to cook for 12-15 minutes, or until the fruit is tender.

2. Remove the pan from the heat and set aside to cool to around room temperature.

3. When cooled add the freshly squeezed lemon juice, zest and Calvados. Stir well to combine.

4. Put in the refrigerator to chill for 2-3 hours before transferring to an ice cream maker and freezing in accordance with the manufacturer's instructions.

Beer Sorbet

Sweet meets sour in yeast infused sorbet.

Servings: 4

Total Time: 2hours 30mins

Ingredients:

- 1 pound mixed stone fruit (cherries, peaches, plums)
- ¾ cup sugar
- ⅓ cup light corn syrup
- ¾ cup lambic beer (chilled)

Directions:

1. First peel and pit the fruit. Place the mixed fruit in a food blender and blitz until silky.

2. In a 3 quart saucepan combine the fruit puree, sugar and corn syrup. Bring to a simmer, stirring well to ensure that the sugar is completely dissolved. Remove the pan from the heat, allow to cool at room temperature before placing in the refrigerator for 2-3 hours to chill.

3. Using a mesh sieve, strain the chilled mixture into a large bowl. Add the lambic beer and place back into the refrigerator to chill.

4. Transfer the sorbet mixture to an ice cream maker and freeze in accordance with the manufacturer's instructions. You need to achieve a soft whipped cream consistency.

5. Put the sorbet into an airtight container, lay a piece of greaseproof paper on top and cover with an airtight lid.

6. Freeze in the coldest section of the freezer for 4-6 hours.

Berry Merlot Sorbet

Fruity dry wine and fresh berries make the perfect adult sorbet.

Portions: 8

Total Time: 8hours 40mins

Ingredients:

- 1 cup white sugar
- ¾ cup cold water
- 1 bottle fruity Merlot
- 1 cup fresh blueberries
- 2 cups fresh raspberries

Directions:

1. In a saucepan, add the sugar, water and merlot. Bring to a boil for a minute and stir well until the sugar has dissolved. Immediately take off the heat and add in the fresh berries. Cover with a lid and set aside to steep for an hour.

2. Pour the syrup into a blender and blitz until smooth. Strain into a mixing bowl, using the back of a spoon to mash any berry pieces against the strainer to give as much juice as possible.

3. Place in the refrigerator and chill for 2-3 hours.

4. Add into an ice cream maker to churn (according to manufacturer's instructions).

5. Transfer to a square baking dish and freeze for 3-4 hours until firm.

Bloody Mary Sorbet

This sorbet is more of an aperitif than a treat or dessert. It is especially delicious served with cheese and crackers.

Servings: 6-8

Total Time: 12hours 30mins

Ingredients:

- 5 ounces granulated sugar
- 5 ounces cold water
- 1 English cucumber (peeled, deseeded)
- 1 shallot (peeled)
- I large pepper (deseeded)
- 16 ounces ripe plum tomatoes (quartered)
- 5 tbsp. vodka
- 5 tbsp. lemon juice
- 5 tbsp. tomato puree

- 1 tsp hot sauce
- 1 tsp Worcestershire sauce
- Salt
- Ground black pepper
- Celery stalks (for garnish)

Directions:

1. In a small saucepan over a medium heat simmer the sugar along with cold water. When the sugar has completely dissolved, increase the heat and boil until thickened, this should take around 4-5 minutes. Set aside to cool for 8-10 minutes.

2. Roughly chop the cucumber, shallot and pepper. Put the chopped vegetables into a food blender and blitz until fine. Add the quartered tomatoes and blitz. Strain the mixture, using a coarse metal sieve over a large jug.

3. Add the syrup to the jug and mix to combine. Strain the mixture through a fine mesh sieve. Pour into an airtight freezer container and freeze for 8 hours. Remove from the freezer and allow to thaw for no more than 30 minutes.

4. Add the sorbet to a food blender and blitz until smooth. Transfer back to the freezer for another 2-3 hours.

5. Remove from the freezer 10-15 mins before serving. Serve in a chilled glass and garnish with celery.

Cheat's Cava Sorbet

Rustle up a quick sorbet for a dinner party using this fast track recipe. Your guests need never know!

Servings: 8-10

Total Time: 20mins

Ingredients:

- 1 quart ready-made lemon sorbet
- Juice of ½ lemon
- 1 bottle of Spanish Cava

Directions:

1. First, remove the store-bought sorbet from the freezer and allow to soften.

2. In a large mixing bowl, beat the sorbet along with the freshly squeezed lemon juice and the Cava. Beat until silky.

3. Pour the mixture into a dessert bowl and freeze.

Chocolate Porter Sorbet

Porter beer gives a deep malty flavor to this decadent bittersweet chocolate sorbet.

Portions: 8

Total Time: 8hours 40mins

Ingredients:

- 1½ cups cold water
- 1 cup white sugar
- ¾ cup cocoa powder (Dutch-process unsweetened)
- ¼ tsp sea salt
- 6 ounces 60% cocoa chocolate (semisweet)
- ¾ cup any brand Porter
- ½ tsp vanilla essence

Directions:

1. In a saucepan, add the water, white sugar, cocoa powder and sea salt. Bring to a boil for one minute and stir well until the sugar has dissolved. Take off the heat.

2. Add in the semisweet chocolate and stir well until it melts completely. Pour in the porter and vanilla essence, mix gently until all ingredients are well combined.

3. Place in the refrigerator and chill for 2-3 hours.

4. Add into an ice cream maker to churn (according to manufacturer's instructions).

5. Transfer to a square baking dish and freeze for 3-4 hours until firm.

Coconut Rum Choc Chip Sorbet

Dairy free coconut milk makes this indulgent sorbet super creamy and smooth.

Portions: 8-10

Total Time: 8hours 40mins

Ingredients:

- 30 ounces full-fat coconut milk (chilled and well shaken)
- ¾ cup simple sugar syrup
- 2 tbsp. dark rum
- 2½ ounces dark chocolate chips

Directions:

1. In a mixing bowl, add the milk and sugar syrup. Whisk until well combined. Add the rum and give a final stir.

2. Place in the refrigerator and chill for 2-3 hours.

3. Add into an ice cream maker to churn (according to manufacturer's instructions). Halfway through churning add in the chocolate chips.

4. Transfer to a square baking dish and freeze for 3-4 hours until firm.

Festive Cranberry Sorbet

Looking for a refreshing way to finish a heavy holiday meal? Or even a palette cleanser between courses? Then this is the sorbet for you.

Portions: 10

Total Time: 8hours 50mins

Ingredients:

- 1½ cups fresh cranberries
- 1 cup cold water
- ¾ cup white sugar
- 1 stick cinnamon

- ½ tsp ground cardamom
- 1½ cups pomegranate juice
- 1 tbsp. vodka*

Directions:

1. In a saucepan, add the cranberries, cold water, white sugar, cinnamon and cardamom. Bring to a boil for one minute and stir well until the sugar has dissolved. Immediately take off the heat and allow to sit at room temperature for half an hour to steep.

2. Remove the cinnamon stick and transfer the mixture to a blender. Blitz until smooth. Strain the puree into a mixing bowl and add the pomegranate juice and vodka. Stir well to combine.

3. Place in the refrigerator and chill for 2-3 hours.

4. Add into an ice cream maker to churn (according to manufacturer's instructions).

5. Transfer to a square baking dish and freeze for 3-4 hours until firm.

*The vodka here is included solely to improve texture and scoop ability. For a kid-friendly version you can omit the vodka but the sorbet may be a little more difficult to scoop and serve.

G&T Sorbet

Your friends will be so impressed when you offer them this delicious sorbet. Serve in martini glasses and garnish with a slice of lemon or lime.

Servings: 4-6

Total Time: 10hours 20mins

Ingredients:

- ½ cup water
- ½ cup sugar
- Juice and zest of 2 limes
- ½ cup gin
- 2½ cups tonic water

Directions:

1. In a small saucepan over medium heat, make a syrup by heating the water along with the sugar. Stir until the sugar has completely dissolved.

2. Remove the pan from the heat and the lime juice and zest. Set to one side to cool, before adding the gin and tonic water. Using a mesh sieve strain and discard any zest.

3. Transfer the strained sorbet mixture to your ice cream maker and freeze in accordance with the manufacturer's instructions, usually around 10-15 minutes.

4. Put the sorbet in an airtight container in the freezer and allow to freeze overnight.

Lemon, Mango and Raspberry Sorbet

Two-layer sorbet guaranteed to give you your 5-a-day.

Servings: 4

Total Time: 9hours 30mins

Ingredients:

- 1 large ripe mango
- 2 tbsp. water
- 4 tbsp. lemon juice
- 2 tbsp. sugar
- ½ tsp ground cinnamon
- ¼ tsp ground cilantro
- 4 ounces sugar
- ½ cup water
- 6 ounces frozen raspberries (thawed, divided)
- 2 tbsp. lemon juice
- 5 ounces sparkling wine

Directions:

1. First peel and pit the mango. Cut the flesh away and slice, and collect the juices. In a food blender puree the mango and juice along with 2 tablespoons of cold water and lemon juice.

2. Strain through a mesh sieve into a large bowl, add the sugar, ground cinnamon, and cilantro and stir to combine. Pour the mixture into a shallow metal baking pan and place in the freezer for 2-3 hours. Stir every 20 minutes in order to prevent the formation of ice crystals.

3. In a small pan, simmer the sugar along with ½ cup of water, for around 12-15 minutes. Set the pan aside to cool. Put a handful of thawed raspberries to one side. Puree the remaining thawed berries along with the lemon juice. Strain the mixture through a fine mesh sieve, discard any seeds. Add the sparkling wine and sugar syrup.

4. Pour the mixture into a shallow bowl and freeze for 3-4 hours, stirring to prevent the formation of ice crystals.

5. When you are ready to serve, combine both flavors together and stir. Garnish with raspberries.

Minted Pineapple Champagne Sorbet

Fresh mint brings a refreshing note to this sophisticated Champagne sorbet.

Portions: 8-10

Total Time: 8hours 40mins

Ingredients:

- ½ fresh medium pineapple (peeled, chopped)
- 8 tbsp. white sugar
- ¼ cup cold water
- ¼ cup good quality Champagne
- 1 tbsp. fresh mint (finely chopped)

Directions:

1. Add the fruit and sugar into a blender and blitz until you have a smooth puree.

2. Add in the water and Champagne. Pulse until just combined. Toss in the mint and pulse again.

3. Pour the mixture into a square baking dish and refrigerate for 3 hours.

4. Transfer the sorbet to an ice cream freezer and freeze using manufacturer's instructions until firm.

5. Scoop and serve!

Mojito Sorbet

The rum in this recipe allows the dessert to have a slightly softer consistency than regular sorbets.

Servings: 16

Total Time: 1hour 25mins

Ingredients:

- 1 cup cold water
- 1 cup white sugar
- ½ cup mint leaves (packed)
- ¼ cup grated lime zest
- 1 cup freshly squeezed lime juice
- 1 ½ cups citrus flavor sparkling water
- 2 tbsp. rum

Directions:

1. In a small saucepan over medium heat, combine the cold water, sugar and mint and stir until the sugar is totally dissolved. Bring the mixture to the boil. Reduce the heat and allow to simmer for 4-5 minutes. Set the mixture to one side to cool. Strain using a mesh sieve and discard the mint leaves.

2. Pour the mint mixture, lime zest, lime juice, citrus water, and rum into a large bowl and stir well to combine. Pour into an ice cream maker and process according to the manufacturer's instructions.

3. Serve at once for a softer consistency, or freeze in an airtight container with a lid for a regular frozen sorbet.

Pink Grapefruit, Grand Marnier and Lavender Sorbet

You will probably need 6 whole grapefruits to make this sorbet. It is well worth it though – it's refreshing and thirst quenching.

Servings: 4-6

Total Time: 7hours 15mins

Ingredients:

- Zest 1 pink grapefruit
- 1 tsp fresh lavender flowers or leaves
- 1 cup sugar
- 4 cups freshly squeezed grapefruit juice
- 1 tbsp. lemon juice
- 1 tbsp. Grand Marnier

Directions:

1. With a vegetable peeler, remove the zest from the peel of 1 pink grapefruit, and coarsely chop the grapefruit zest.

2. In a food blender, combine the zest, lavender flowers and cup of sugar. Blitz until the zest is finely chopped. Add the grapefruit juice to the mixture along with the lemon juice, and Grand Marnier. Stir well to combine.

3. Transfer the mixture to an ice cream maker and churn in accordance with the manufacturer's instructions.

4. Freeze for 3-4 hours until firm.

Rosé Watermelon Sorbet

Our new favorite way to enjoy sweet rose wine! Perfect for girl's night in, drop a scoop in your favorite glass of wine for the ultimate spritzer.

Portions: 6-8

Total Time: 8hours 40mins

Ingredients:

- 1 cup rosé wine
- ⅓ cup white sugar
- 2 cups fresh watermelon juice

Directions:

1. In a small saucepan over medium heat, add the rosé wine and sugar. As soon as the sugar dissolves, take off the heat.

2. Pour the rose syrup into a bowl along with the watermelon juice and chill for 4-5 hours.

3. Transfer the chilled mixture into an ice cream maker and (according to manufacturer's instructions) freeze until firm.

Rum & Pineapple Sorbet

The beauty of this recipe is that you can serve this sorbet right away. It has a looser consistency but is really refreshing.

Servings: 6

Total Time: 30mins

Ingredients:

- 30-32 ice cubes
- 1 ripe large pineapple (peeled, chopped)
- 9 ounces powdered sugar
- Freshly squeezed juice of 1 lemon
- 1 egg white
- 2 tbsp. dark rum
-

Directions:

1. Using a high powered food blender to grind the ice cubes; aim for snow like consistency.

2. Transfer the snow into a large plastic mixing bowl or jug and set to one side.

3. Blend the remaining 5 ingredients for 1½ minutes, or until a smooth mixture has been made. Add the snow and blitz for 2-3 seconds more.

4. You can serve this sorbet straight away or place it in an airtight container and freeze. Just remember to stir every 20 minutes or so until the sorbet is frozen solid.

Sparkling Pear Sorbet

A light and refreshing sorbet, the perfect way to finish a dinner party.

Portions: 8-10

Total Time: 8hours 40mins

Ingredients:

- 1½ cups Prosecco
- ¾ cup white sugar
- 1 tbsp. light corn syrup
- 1½ cups pear juice
- 2 tbsp. freshly squeezed lemon juice

Directions:

1. In a saucepan, add the Prosecco, white sugar and light corn syrup. Bring to a boil slowly and stir well until the sugar has dissolved. Immediately take off the heat and pour into a mixing bowl. Pour in the pear and lemon juice and stir well.

2. Place in the refrigerator and chill for 2-3 hours.

3. Add into an ice cream maker to churn (according to manufacturer's instructions).

4. Transfer to a square baking dish and freeze for 3-4 hours until firm.

Spiked Grape Sorbet

Sweet grape sorbet spiked with a shot of vodka! This is definitely one for the grown-ups.

Portions: 10

Total Time: 8hours 40mins

Ingredients:

- 3½ pounds fresh seedless grapes (halved)
- 3 tbsp. cold water
- ¼ cup corn syrup
- 1 tbsp. good quality vodka

Directions:

1. In a saucepan, add the grapes and water. Cover with a lid and cook until the grapes (skin) 'burst' and the fruit is cooked through and soft.

2. Strain the fruit into a mixing bowl. Use a spatula to 'press' the fruit against the strainer to pass through as much pulp as possible. Add the corn syrup and vodka. Stir until well combined.

3. Place in the refrigerator and chill for 2-3 hours.

4. Add into an ice cream maker to churn (according to manufacturer's instructions).

5. Transfer to a square baking dish and freeze for 3-4 hours until firm.

Tangerine and Prosecco Sorbet

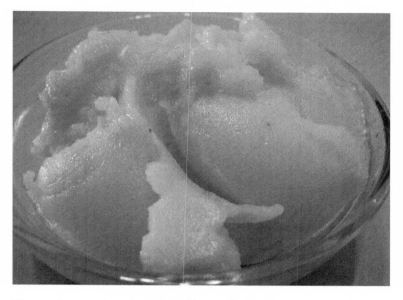

Tangerines pair exceptionally well with Prosecco and are a welcome alternative to oranges.

Portions: 6-8

Total Time: 10hours 10mins

Ingredients:

- ¾ cup white sugar
- ¾ cup cold water
- 2 cups of freshly squeezed tangerine juice (strained, chilled)
- 1 cup Prosecco (chilled)
- 1 tbsp. tangerine peel (finely grated)

Directions:

1. In a small saucepan combine the white sugar and cold water over med-high heat. Stir until the sugar totally dissolves. Increase the heat and bring the syrup to the boil. Transfer to a medium-sized bowl and allow to chill for 2-3 hours.

2. Add the tangerine juice, chilled Prosecco and tangerine peel to the syrup, Whisk well to blend. Transfer the mixture onto an ice cream maker and process in accordance with the manufacturer's instructions.

3. Transfer the sorbet to a suitable freezer container. Cover with a tight-fitting lid and place in the freezer overnight.

4. Serve frozen.

Watermelon Sorbet with Prosecco

This sorbet can be stored in the freezer for up to 8 weeks.

Servings: 4

Total Time: 12hours 45mins

Ingredients:

- ½ cup cold water
- ½ cup sugar
- 1 stalk lemongrass (halved lengthways)
- ¼ watermelon (deseeded, pureed)
- Juice of 1 lime
- 1 egg white (medium)
- 2 cups Prosecco
- Mint leaves

Directions:

1. In a small saucepan heat the water, sugar and lemongrass together until the sugar is totally dissolved. Set the pan to one side and allow the syrup to cool. Remove the lemongrass and discard.

2. Mix the cool syrup along with the watermelon puree and freshly squeezed lime juice. Pour the mixture into a wide container and freeze for 10-12 hours. You will need to stir it ever half an hour for the first 8 hours. After 2 hours of freezing, whisk the egg white until it is stiff and mix it into the sorbet.

3. When you are ready to serve, put 2-3 spoonfuls of the watermelon sorbet into 4 glasses and fill to the top with Prosecco. Garnish with mint.

4. The sorbet will keep for up to 8 weeks if stored in the freezer in an airtight container with a lid.

Whiskey Sorbet

A grown-up sorbet for the long summer evenings.

Servings: 10-12

Total Time: 10hours 20mins

Ingredients:

- 4 cups cold water
- 4 ounces whiskey (divided)
- 1-2 tablespoons freshly grated lemon zest
- 2 cups freshly squeezed lemon juice (cold)
- 1 ½ cups sugar
- ½ cup fresh mint (finely chopped)

Directions:

1. In a small saucepan over med-high heat, bring the cold water, sugar, lemon zest and 2 ounces of whiskey to a boil. Reduce the heat to low and simmer the syrup for 4-5 minutes. Stir, until the sugar has totally dissolved.

2. Remove the pan from the heat, add the fresh mint and stir well. Allow the mixture to cool to room temperature. Transfer to the refrigerator and chill overnight.

3. Strain the mixture through a mesh sieve and discard any solids. Press down to extract all the juice out. Add the freshly squeezed lemon juice and the remaining 2 ounces of whiskey. Stir well, before processing in an ice cream maker in accordance with the manufacturer's instructions.

UNDER 21's

Alligator Pear (Avocado) Soft-Serve Sorbet

The perfect palate cleanser to serve after a particularly spicy entrée.

Servings: 4

Total Time: 6hours 30mins

Ingredients:

- ¾ cup avocado (peeled, pitted, cut into chunks)
- ½ cup agave syrup
- ½ cup light coconut milk
- ¼ cup freshly squeezed lime juice
- 2 tsp lime zest (finely grated)

Directions:

1. In a food blender, puree the chunked avocado until almost smooth. Scrape the sides of the blender jug, and add the syrup, once again puree. While the motor is still running, a little at a time, add the light coconut milk. Blitz until you have a smooth consistency. Add the freshly squeezed lime juice and grated zest. Blitz until silky.

2. Transfer the sorbet mixture to an airtight container and place in the refrigerator to chill, for between 4-6 hours.

3. Put the mixture in an ice cream maker and process in accordance with the manufacturer's instructions.

4. Serve immediately with a soft-serve sorbet.

Creamy Prickly Pear and Coconut Sorbet

Prickly pears are a delicious and unusual fruit hailing from the South West of America. Creamy coconut is the perfect partner to this tart yet sweet fruit,

Portions: 8

Total Time: 8hours 40mins

Ingredients:

- 15 ounces canned full-fat coconut milk (well shaken)
- ¾ cup prickly pear syrup
- Freshly squeezed juice of ½ a lime
- Pinch sea salt

Directions:

1. Whisk the coconut milk until smooth in a mixing bowl. Add in the remaining ingredients and continue to mix until well combined and smooth.

2. Place in the refrigerator and chill for 2-3 hours.

3. Add into an ice cream maker to churn (according to manufacturer's instructions).

4. Transfer to a square baking dish and freeze for 3-4 hours until firm.

Cucumber Cantaloupe Sorbet

Fresh green flavors make for a crisp and refreshing sorbet.

Portions: 8-10

Total Time: 8hours 40mins

Ingredients:

- 1 cup pureed cucumber
- 2 cups pureed cantaloupe
- 1 cup simple sugar syrup
- ¼ tsp sea salt

Directions:

1. Add all ingredients into a blender and blitz until totally combined.

2. Place in the refrigerator and chill for 2-3 hours.

3. Add into an ice cream maker to churn (according to manufacturer's instructions).

4. Transfer to a square baking dish and freeze for 3-4 hours until firm.

Hibiscus and Cardamom Mango Sorbet

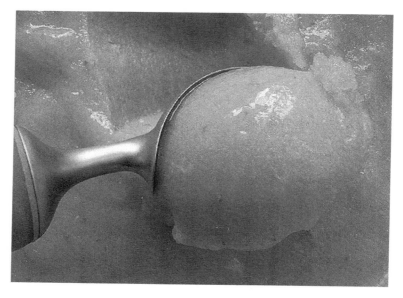

Both floral and aromatic with a burst of tropical mango this is the ultimate summer treat. Enjoy on a summer evening sitting in the backyard with your feet up.

Portions: 10

Total Time: 8hours 40mins

Ingredients:

- 2 cups mango puree
- ⅔ cup white sugar
- ⅔ cup cold water
- Juice of 2½ fresh limes
- ¼ tsp sea salt
- ¼ tsp hibiscus powder
- ½ tsp ground cardamom

Directions:

1. Combine all ingredients in a blender and blitz until smooth.

2. Place in the refrigerator and chill for 2-3 hours.

3. Add into an ice cream maker to churn (according to manufacturer's instructions).

4. Transfer to a square baking dish and freeze for 3-4 hours until firm.

Kiwi and Strawberry Sorbet

Tangy kiwi and sweet strawberries come together to make a juicy sorbet that everyone will love.

Portions: 6

Total Time: 12hours 40mins

Ingredients:

- 1 cup cold water
- 1 cup white sugar
- 3½ cups fresh strawberries
- 1½ cups fresh kiwi (chopped)

Directions:

1. In a saucepan over med-high heat, add the water, sugar and 2 cups of the strawberries.

2. Simmer for half an hour, until the sugar totally dissolves and the liquid has reduced.

3. Strain the mixture into a bowl and allow to cool before adding into a blender with the remaining strawberries and kiwi.

4. Blitz until smooth and transfer to a square baking dish. Place in the freezer for 12 hours.

5. Allow to stand at room temperature for 7-8 minutes before serving in scoops.

Kumquat Sorbet

Kumquats often go underappreciated and underused. These little orange fruits are bursting with juicy bittersweet flavor, making them ideal for sorbet.

Portions: 10

Total Time: 8hours 40mins

Ingredients:

- 1½ pounds fresh kumquats
- Water
- 2 cups simple sugar syrup

Directions:

1. In a saucepan, add the kumquats and cover with water. Bring the mixture to a boil. Take off the heat, drain away the water then repeat another 2 times.*

2. Add the kumquats into a blender along with half of the simple sugar syrup. Blitz until you have a smooth puree. Strain the mixture into a bowl. Stir in the remaining simple sugar syrup.

3. Place in the refrigerator and chill for 2-3 hours.

4. Add into an ice cream maker to churn (according to manufacturer's instructions).

5. Transfer to a square baking dish and freeze for 3-4 hours until firm.

*This step is important as it helps to reduce the bitterness of the fruit.

Lemon Sorbet with Blackberry Topping

A quick dessert to whip up packed with citrus and berry flavors.

Servings: 10

Total Time: 1hour 10mins

Ingredients:

- 1 pound frozen unsweetened blackberries (unthawed)
- 5 tbsp. sugar
- 3 pints ready-made lemon sorbet

Directions:

1. Place the unthawed, frozen blackberries in a large mixing bowl. Sprinkle the sugar over the blackberries. Allow to stand until the berries are slightly thawed and cold, this should take about 60 minutes. Using a metal fork mash the blackberries.

2. Cover and freeze until needed.

3. Spoon the store-bought lemon sorbet into large glasses. Top with blackberry sauce.

Lime and Honeydew Melon Sorbet

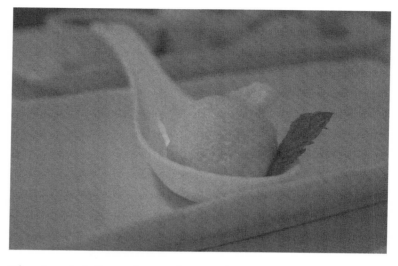

Floral and delicate honeydew melon meets zesty lime for a light and refreshing sorbet.

Portions: 6

Total Time: 12hours 40mins

Ingredients:

- 1 cup cold water
- 1 cup white sugar
- 1 cup fresh squeezed lime juice
- 1 tbsp. lime zest
- 2 cups fresh honeydew melon (chopped)

Directions:

1. In a saucepan over medium heat, add the water, sugar, half of the lime juice and all of the zest.

2. Simmer for half an hour, until the sugar totally dissolves and the liquid has reduced.

3. Strain the mixture into a bowl and allow to cool before adding into a blender with the remaining lime juice and honeydew melon.

4. Blitz until smooth and transfer to a square baking dish. Place in the freezer for 12 hours.

5. Allow to stand at room temperature for 7-8 minutes before serving in scoops.

Orange and Carrot Sorbet

Sweet carrots add depth of flavor to this vibrant citrus sorbet.

Portions: 8-10

Total Time: 8hours 40mins

Ingredients:

- ⅓ cup cold water
- 1 cup white sugar
- 2 cups carrot juice
- 2 tbsp. freshly squeezed lemon juice
- 1½ tbsp. orange extract

Directions:

1. In a saucepan, add the water and sugar. Bring to a boil and stir well until the sugar has dissolved. Take off the heat and allow to sit at room temperature for half an hour to cool a little.

2. Add in the remaining ingredients, stir well to combine.

3. Place in the refrigerator and chill for 2-3 hours.

4. Add into an ice cream maker to churn (according to manufacturer's instructions).

5. Transfer to a square baking dish and freeze for 3-4 hours until firm.

Papaya Lime Sorbet

If you can get your hands on one, Hawaiian papaya is known to be the sweetest and juiciest.

Portions: 10-12

Total Time: 8hours 40mins

Ingredients:

- 2 pounds fresh papaya (peeled, deseeded, chopped)
- ⅔ cup white sugar
- ¼ cup cold water
- Juice of 3 fresh limes
- ¼ tsp sea salt

Directions:

1. Add all ingredients into a blender and blitz until smooth.

2. Place in the refrigerator and chill for 2-3 hours.

3. Add into an ice cream maker to churn (according to manufacturer's instructions). Serve!*

*Most sorbets are placed in the freezer after churning; however, this sorbet tastes better a little less set. If you are not ready to serve it right away; freeze it but allow it to stand at room temperature for 10-12 minutes before serving.

Peachy Earl Grey Tea Sorbet

Early Gray is a classic English black tea with floral citrusy notes of orange and bergamot. It blends beautifully with fresh peaches in this summery sorbet.

Portions: 10-12

Total Time: 8hours 40mins

Ingredients:

- 1½ pounds fresh peaches (skin removed, pitted, chopped)
- 1⅛ cups cold water
- 3 Earl Grey (any brand) tea bags
- 1⅛ cups white sugar

Directions:

1. In a saucepan, add the chopped peaches, cold water and Earl Grey tea bags. Bring to a boil slowly, then reduce to a simmer for 8-9 minutes. Take off the heat and remove the tea bags. Add in the sugar and stir well until the sugar dissolves.

2. Transfer the puree to a blender and blitz until smooth.

3. Place in the refrigerator and chill for 2-3 hours.

4. Add into an ice cream maker to churn (according to manufacturer's instructions).

5. Transfer to a square baking dish and freeze for 3-4 hours until firm.

Peanut Butter and Cola Sorbet

Fizzy cola, molasses and peanut butter – sweet and buttery, a winning combination.

Servings: 6

Total Time: 8hours 20mins

Ingredients:

- 1½ cups regular cola (any brand)
- ½ cup light clear corn syrup
- ½ cup smooth peanut butter
- ¼ cup sugar
- 1 tbsp. molasses
- ¼ tsp vanilla extract
- Salt to taste
- ½ cup roasted and salted peanuts (chilled in freezer)

Directions:

1. In a food blender, combine the cola, syrup, peanut butter, sugar, molasses and vanilla extract. Biz until silky, this should take around 30 seconds. Add a little salt to taste. Chill in the refrigerator until cold, approx. 3-4 hours.

2. Put the mixture in an ice cream maker and freeze in accordance with the manufacturer's instructions. Add the peanuts at the very last moment.

3. Transfer to a container with a lid and freeze for up to 4 hours before you are ready to serve.

Pekoe Tea Sorbet

Tea is ordinarily a refreshing drink on a hot day but as sorbet it's a real cool down treat.

Servings: 6

Total Time: 2hours 10mins

Ingredients:

- 1 cup white sugar
- ½ cup water
- 1 sprig fresh mint (leaves removed, stem discarded)
- 2 cups brewed orange pekoe tea
- Juice of ½ lemon

Directions:

1. In a small saucepan over medium heat combine the white sugar, along with the water and mint leaves. Cook and stir, until the sugar has totally dissolved and the mixture has the consistency of syrup. Remove the saucepan from the heat. Strain, using a mesh sieve and discard the leave. Set the syrup aside to cool at room temperature for around, 25 minutes.

2. In a medium size bowl combine the brewed orange pekoe tea with the lemon juice. Add the syrup and stir well. Transfer to the refrigerator to chill for 30 minutes.

3. When chilled, pour the sorbet mixture into an ice cream maker and freeze in accordance with the manufacturer's instructions.

Pina Colada Sorbet

A creamy, pineapple flavor sorbet.

Servings: 8

Total Time: 3hours 25mins

Ingredients:

- 1½ cups white sugar
- 1½ cups water
- 20 ounces can crushed pineapple (drained)
- 13½ ounces can coconut milk
- ¼ cup lime juice

Directions:

1. Add the white sugar and water to a small saucepan and over medium heat bring to the boil, for approx. 1-2 minutes until the sugar has totally dissolved. Set aside to cool.

2. In a food blender blitz the pineapple until it is frothy and smooth. In a large size mixing bowl, whisk the syrup along with the pineapple puree, coconut milk and freshly squeezed lime juice.

3. Transfer to the refrigerator for 2-3 hours, until chilled.

Pineapple and Basil Sorbet

A perfect pairing.

Servings: 12-14

Total Time: 9hours 20mins

Ingredients:

- 1 fresh pineapple (peeled, cored, cut into chunks)
- ½ cup white sugar
- ½ cup pineapple juice
- ¼ cup basil leaves

Directions:

1. In a food blender, blitz the pineapple, white sugar, pineapple juice and basil until silky. Place in the refrigerator to chill for 1-2 hours.

2. Place the mixture in an ice cream maker and process according to manufacturer's directions. Transfer to a container with a lid and freeze overnight.

Pineapple Mango Sorbet

This fruity tropical sorbet will have your dreaming of Caribbean beaches.

Portions: 6

Total Time: 12hours 40mins

Ingredients:

- 1 cup cold water
- 1 cup white sugar
- 3 cups fresh mango (chopped)
- 1½ cups fresh pineapple (chopped)

Directions:

1. In a small saucepan over medium heat, add the water, sugar and half of the mango.

2. Simmer for half an hour, until the sugar totally dissolves and the liquid has reduced.

3. Strain the mixture into a bowl and allow to cool before adding into a blender with the remaining mango and pineapple.

4. Blitz until smooth and transfer to a square baking dish. Place in the freezer for 12 hours.

5. Allow to stand at room temperature for 7-8 minutes before serving in scoops.

Raspberry Lemonade Sorbet

Sweet raspberries and tangy lemon make the perfect pairing.

Portions: 6

Total Time: 12hours 40mins

Ingredients:

- 1 cup cold water
- 1 cup white sugar
- 3½ cups fresh raspberries
- ½ cup fresh squeezed lemon juice

Directions:

1. In a small saucepan over medium heat, add the water, sugar and 2 cups of the raspberries.

2. Simmer for half an hour, until the sugar totally dissolves and the liquid has reduced.

3. Strain the mixture into a bowl and allow to cool before adding into a blender with the remaining raspberries and lemon juice.

4. Blitz until smooth and transfer to a square baking dish. Place in the freezer for 12 hours.

5. Allow to stand at room temperature for 7-8 minutes before serving in scoops.

Red Plum Sorbet

Jewel toned plums make for a sweet yet delightfully tart sorbet.

Portions: 10-12

Total Time: 8hours 40mins

Ingredients:

- 2 pounds fresh red plums (destoned, chopped)
- 1½ cups cold water
- 1½ cups white sugar

Directions:

1. Into a saucepan bring to boil the plums and water. Turn the heat down to a simmer and cook for 3-9 minutes. Take off the heat and add in the sugar. Stir continuously until the sugar dissolves.

2. Transfer the puree to a blender and blitz until smooth.

3. Place in the refrigerator and chill for 2-3 hours.

4. Add into an ice cream maker to churn (according to manufacturer's instructions). Halfway through churning add in the chocolate chips.

5. Transfer to a square baking dish and freeze for 3-4 hours until firm.

Simple Mint Sorbet

You can serve this sorbet either as a dessert or in between courses.

Servings: 2

Total Time: 4hours 25mins

- Ingredients:
- 1 cup cold water
- 1 cup white sugar
- 4 cups fresh mint leaves

Directions:

1. In a saucepan, over medium heat, combine the water along with the sugar. Cook and stir until the sugar has totally dissolved. Bring to a boil. Turn down to a simmer and continue to heat for 4-5 minutes. Remove from the heat and allow the syrup to cool at room temperature.

2. In a large pan, bring 2 quarts of water to the boil. Prepare a suitable ice water bath and put to one side. Add the mint to the boiling water for around 40 seconds. Drain, using a sieve and place the mint in the ice water bath. Draining and squeezing out excess water.

3. Place the mint in a food blender along with the syrup and blitz until silky. You can add a little more syrup if you feel it is necessary.

4. Pour the mixture into an ice cream maker and freeze in accordance with the manufacturer's instructions.

5. Store in the freezer in an airtight container for no more than 72 hours.

Spanish Tarragon and Satsuma Sorbet

The majority of tarragon sold in supermarkets is French. Spanish tarragon has a more intense, almost spicy taste with subtle flavors of anise. Look out for it in your local delicatessen or specialist supermarket.

Portions: 10-12

Total Time: 8hours 40mins

Ingredients:

- 3 cups fresh Satsuma juice
- 1 cup white sugar
- 3 ounces Spanish tarragon leaves
- 1 tbsp. orange extract

Directions:

1. In a saucepan, add half of the Satsuma juice and sugar. Bring to a boil, whilst stirring until the sugar dissolves. Remove from the heat and toss in the Spanish tarragon. Set the mixture aside, covered, for 20 minutes to steep.

2. Add in the orange extract and remaining Satsuma juice, stir to combine. Place in the refrigerator and chill for 2-3 hours.

3. Add into an ice cream maker to churn (according to manufacturer's instructions).

4. Transfer to a square baking dish and freeze for 3-4 hours until firm.

Author's Afterthoughts

*Thanks ever so much to each of my cherished readers
for investing the time to read this book!*

*I know you could have picked from many other books but
you chose this one. So a big thanks for downloading this
book and reading all the way to the end.*

*If you enjoyed this book or received value from it, I'd like to
ask you for a favor. Please take a few minutes to post an
honest and heartfelt review on Amazon.com. Your support
does make a difference and helps to benefit other people.*

Thanks!

Daniel Humphreys

About the Author

Daniel Humphreys

Many people will ask me if I am German or Norman, and my answer is that I am 100% unique! Joking aside, I owe my cooking influence mainly to my mother who was British! I can certainly make a mean Sheppard's pie, but when it comes to preparing Bratwurst sausages and drinking beer with friends, I am also all in!

I am taking you on this culinary journey with me and hope you can appreciate my diversified background. In my 15 years career as a chef, I never had a dish returned to me by one of clients, so that should say something about me! Actually, I will take that back. My worst critic is my four years old son, who refuses to taste anything that is green color. That shall pass, I am sure.

My hope is to help my children discover the joy of cooking and sharing their creations with their loved ones, like I did all my life. When you develop a passion for cooking and my suspicious is that you have one as well, it usually sticks for life. The best advice I can give anyone as a professional chef is invest. Invest your time, your heart in each meal you are creating. Invest also a little money in good cooking hardware and quality ingredients. But most of all enjoy every meal you prepare with YOUR friends and family!

Made in the
USA
Monee, IL